WITHDRAWN

Stevie Wonder

Published in the United States of America by Cherry Lake Publishing
Ann Arbor, Michigan
www.cherrylakepublishing.com

Reading Adviser: Marla Conn, MS, Ed, Literacy specialist, Read-Ability, Inc.
Book Designer: Jennifer Wahi
Illustrator: Jeff Bane

Photo Credits: ©Dmitrijs Kaminskis/Shutterstock, 5; ©Jen Dunham/Shutterstock, 7; © Bettmann/CORBIS/Sarah W./flickr, 9; ©Nationaal Archief/Photographed by Nijs, Jac. de/Anefo/Component No. 920-8212/Public Domain, 11; ©James R. Martin/Shutterstock, 13, 22; ©Hayk_Shalunts/Shutterstock, 15; ©Susan Montgomery/Shutterstock, 17; ©Krista Kennell/Shutterstock, 19, 23; ©Gustavo Miguel Fernandes/Shutterstock, 21; Jeff Bane, cover, 1, 10, 14, 18

Copyright ©2020 by Cherry Lake Publishing
All rights reserved. No part of this book may be reproduced or utilized in any form or by any means without written permission from the publisher.

Library of Congress Cataloging-in-Publication Data

Names: Sarantou, Katlin, author. | Bane, Jeff, 1957- illustrator.
Title: Stevie Wonder : my itty-bitty bio / by Katlin Sarantou ; illustrated by Jeff Bane.
Description: Ann Arbor : Cherry Lake Publishing, 2019. | Series: My Itty-bitty bio | Audience: K to Grade 3. | Includes bibliographical references and index.
Identifiers: LCCN 2019004211| ISBN 9781534147027 (hardcover) | ISBN 9781534148451 (pdf) | ISBN 9781534149885 (pbk.) | ISBN 9781534151314 (hosted ebook)
Subjects: LCSH: Wonder, Stevie--Juvenile literature. | African American musicians--Biography--Juvenile literature. | Musicians--United States--Biography--Juvenile literature. | Soul musicians--United States--Biography--Juvenile literature. | Rhythm and blues musicians--United States--Biography--Juvenile literature.
Classification: LCC ML3930.W65 S37 2019 | DDC 782.421644092 [B] --dc23
LC record available at https://lccn.loc.gov/2019004211

Printed in the United States of America
Corporate Graphics

About the author: Katlin Sarantou grew up in the cornfields of Ohio. She enjoys reading and dreaming of faraway places.

About the illustrator: Jeff Bane and his two business partners own a studio along the American River in Folsom, California, home of the 1849 Gold Rush. When Jeff's not sketching or illustrating for clients, he's either swimming or kayaking in the river to relax.

I was born in Michigan.
It was 1950.

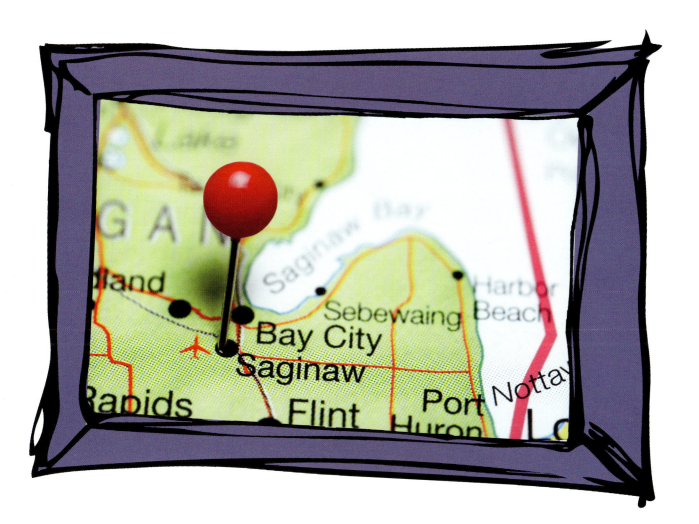

I was born 6 weeks early.

This meant I faced **complications**. I became blind.

What is something that you've had to overcome?

I didn't let my blindness stop me.

I learned to play instruments when I was young.

I played the piano, harmonica, and drums.

I used to **perform** on street corners with a friend.

What do you and your friends like to do together?

I signed with my first **record label** in 1961. I was 11.

I've sold over 100 million records. I've had a lot of success. I've won many awards. I have 25 **Grammys**. I'm in the Rock and Roll Hall of Fame.

I am also an **activist**.

I helped make Martin Luther King Jr.'s birthday a holiday.

Martin Luther King Jr.
January 15, 1929
April 4, 1968

What day would you like to make a holiday?

In 2009, the **United Nations** named me a Messenger of Peace.

I help promote **human rights**.

Today, I still perform my music.

I have made a lasting impact on the music industry.

What would you like to ask me?

1961

1950

Born
1950

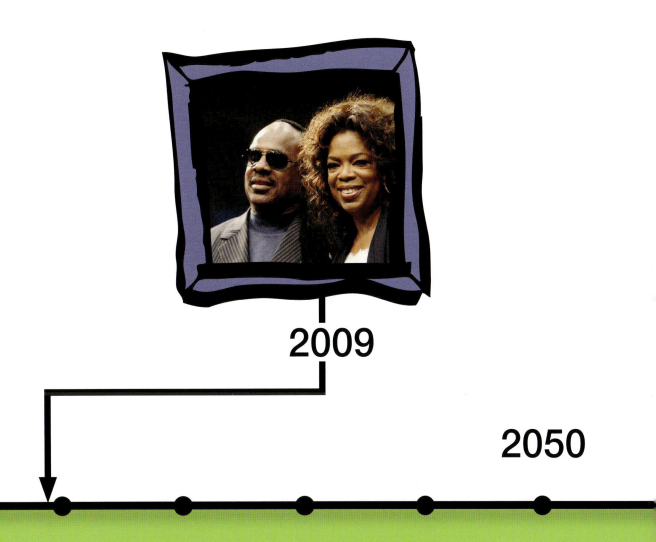

2009

2050

glossary

activist (AK-tiv-ist) a person who works to bring about political or social change

complications (kahm-plih-KAY-shuhnz) conditions that make something difficult

Grammys (GRAM-eez) awards given to people in the music industry

human rights (HYOO-muhn RITES) everyone's right to be treated fairly and to speak freely

perform (pur-FORM) to entertain an audience

record label (REK-urd LAY-buhl) a company that promotes music

United Nations (yoo-NITE-id NAY-shuhnz) an organization of countries that works together toward world peace

index

CONTRA COSTA COUNTY LIBRARY

31901067871022